DANCE

DANCE

Keith Haring

A Bulfinch Press Book
Little, Brown and Company
Boston • New York • London

Dance and music were integral to Keith Haring's creative process. He gave a great deal of thought to how the arts interacted, and the line of his brush conveys the energy and movement of dance, from hip-hop and break dancing to modern dance and ballet.

First edition
Haring, Keith
Love / Keith Haring–1st ed.   7 5 9   HAR
    p. cm.
"A Bulfinch Press book."
ISBN 0-8212-2555-3 (hc.)
1. Haring, Keith–Quotations. 2. Dance in art. I. Title.
NC139.H3A2 1999
741.973–dc21   98–56464

Quotes from the *Keith Haring Journals* used by permission of Viking Penguin, a division of Penguin Books USA Inc.

Bulfinch Press is an imprint and trademark of Little, Brown and Company (Inc.)

Design by Pandiscio, Inc.

PRINTED IN SPAIN   D. L.TO 120-1999

The Keith Haring artwork in this book has been reproduced faithfully; however, the colors of some works have been altered.

THE MUSIC, DANCE, THEATER, AND THE VISUAL ARTS;
THE FORMS OF EXPRESSION, THE ARTS OF HOPE.
THIS IS WHERE I THINK I FIT IN.

I HAD MUSIC HOOKED UP TO A BIG SPEAKER WHILE
I WAS PAINTING. EVERY DAY WAS LIKE A BLOCK PARTY.

SEE, THERE WAS THIS INCREDIBLY RAW ENERGY
IN THE AIR — AND IT LASTED FOR A GOOD TWO
OR THREE YEARS — AND THE ENERGY
WAS CALLED HIP-HOP.

... IT WAS ALMOST LIKE A DIALOGUE GOING ON BACK AND FORTH ... THINGS THAT I WAS SEEING IN DANCES AND LITERALLY PUTTING THEM RIGHT INTO THE WORK ... [THE BREAK DANCERS] KNEW, WHEN THEY SAW IT, RIGHT AWAY WHAT IT WAS.

BREAK DANCING WAS A REAL INSPIRATION...
SO MY DRAWINGS BEGAN HAVING FIGURES SPINNING
ON THEIR HEADS AND TWISTING AROUND.

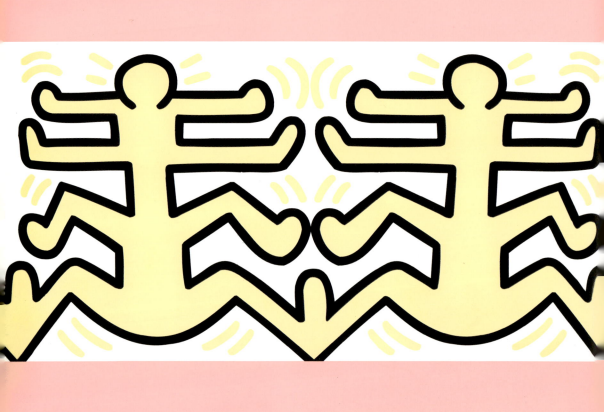

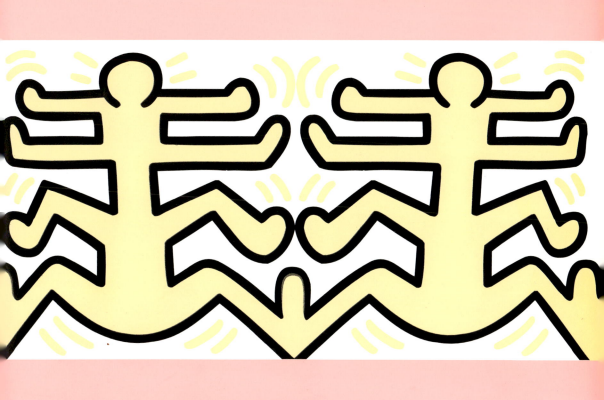

WHEN I HAVE MASTERED THE ABILITY
TO USE BOTH ARMS INTERCHANGEABLY;
WHEN I CAN CONTROL EACH ARM SEPARATELY
AND PERFORM DIFFERENT MOVEMENTS
AT THE SAME TIME, AS A PIANO PLAYER CAN;
WHEN I CAN UNIFY MY MOVEMENTS SO
THAT I CAN PAINT CONSISTENTLY AT A
VERY HIGH RATE OF SPEED ON A VERY
SPONTANEOUS, NATURAL, SPIRITUAL LEVEL;
THEN PERHAPS I WILL HAVE EXHAUSTED
THE POSSIBILITIES OF THE KIND OF
"BODY-INVOLVEMENT" PAINTING I AM
CURRENTLY INVOLVED IN.

FOR ME IT HAS AN INTERESTING FEELING
OF CONFLICT. THE LEFT HAND FIGHTS TO BE
AS CONTROLLED AS THE RIGHT.
THE RIGHT HAND FIGHTS THE LEFT TO
MAKE ALL OF THE IMPORTANT JUDGMENTS
OF LINE. THE TWO HANDS ARE CONSTANTLY
TRYING TO WORK TOGETHER, BUT BECAUSE
THEY ARE SO DISTINCTLY DIFFERENT, THEY
TEND TO STRUGGLE WITH EACH OTHER TO
FIND COMMON GROUND, TO FIND
UNITY/CONSISTENCY.

I BOUGHT THREE BRUSHES THAT ARE
APPROXIMATELY THREE FEET LONG.
IT IS AMAZING TO HOLD THEM
IN YOUR HANDS AND MOVE THEM
ABOUT. I FEEL LIKE I AM DOING A
"CEREMONIAL STICK DANCE."

DANCING WAS REALLY DANCING IN A WAY
TO REACH ANOTHER STATE OF MIND, TO
TRANSCEND BEING HERE AND GETTING
COMMUNALLY TO ANOTHER PLACE.

MOVEMENT AS PAINTING.
PAINTING AS MOVEMENT.

THE PHYSICAL REALITY OF THE
WORLD AS WE KNOW IT IS MOTION.
MOTION ITSELF = MOVEMENT.

LIFE AND DEATH ARE INEVITABLE.
I THINK I'VE HAD A GREAT LIFE
AND EVERY DAY IS A SURPRISE. I'M HAPPY
TO BE ALIVE TODAY.

WHAT I AM PROPOSING, OR WHAT
I AM PRACTICING FOR MYSELF, IS A BODY
OF WORK THAT IS IN CONSTANT MOTION.

NEVER "FINAL," NEVER "FINISHED".

THE IMPORTANCE OF MOVEMENT IS INTENSIFIED
WHEN A PAINTING BECOMES A PERFORMANCE.
THE PERFORMANCE (THE ACT OF PAINTING)
BECOMES AS IMPORTANT AS THE
RESULTING PAINTING.

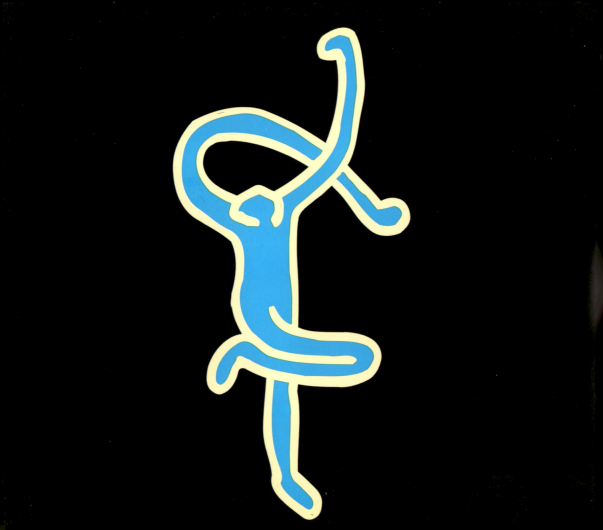

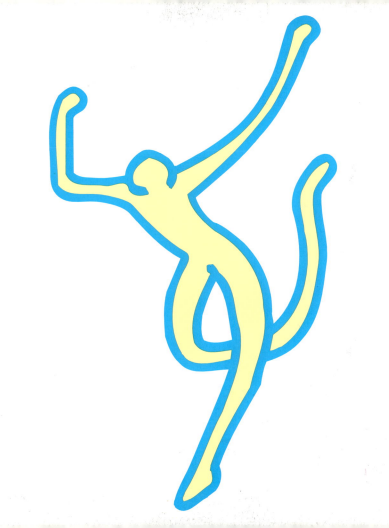

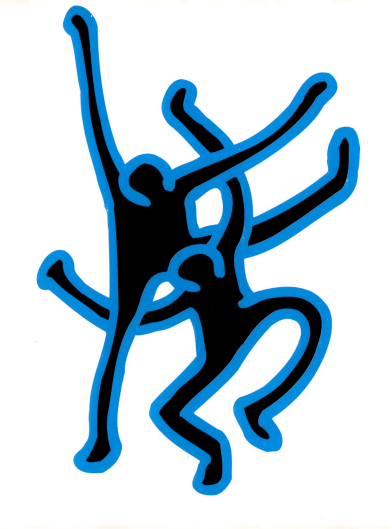

I SHARE THE SAME CONCERNS FOR SPACE AND
MOVEMENT AND STRUCTURE AS CONTEMPORARY
DANCERS. I CONSIDER SPONTANEITY,

IMPROVISATION,

CONTINUITY

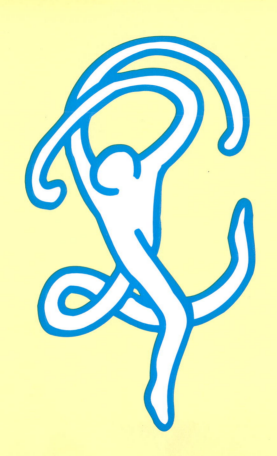

AND HARMONY.

ONE FINAL BOW. MOMENTS LIKE THIS
MAKE ME FALL IN LOVE WITH THIS COUNTRY...
THERE IS A KIND OF POETRY TO ALL LIFE
HERE AND EVERY ACTION SEEMS SYMBOLIC.

EVERYTHING IS CONSTANTLY CHANGING.
EVERY SECOND FROM BIRTH IS SPENT EXPERIENCING;
DIFFERENT SENSATIONS, DIFFERENT INTERJECTIONS,
DIFFERENT DIRECTIONAL VECTORS OF FORCE/ENERGY
CONSTANTLY COMPOSING AND RECOMPOSING
THEMSELVES AROUND YOU.

A MODERN ARTIST HAS TO PRODUCE IMAGES...
HOWEVER, THE ELEMENTS OF CHANCE, AND
MAGIC, AND SPIRIT CANNOT BE SACRIFICED
IN THIS QUEST.

EVERY DRAWING IS A PERFORMANCE
AND A RITUAL.

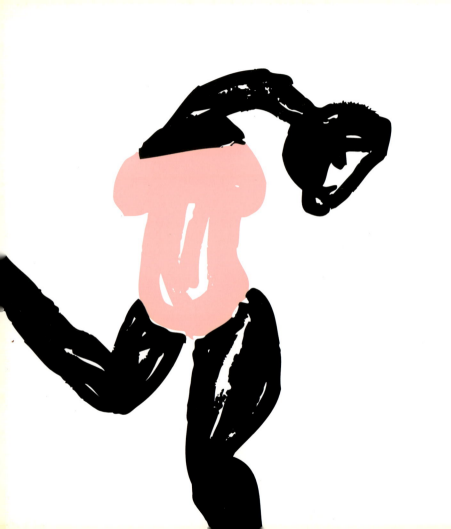

NOTHING IS CHAOTIC.

THE ACT OF CREATION ITSELF IS VERY
CLEAR AND PURE.

THE FREEDOM OF THE ARTIST IS
SYMBOLIC OF THE HUMAN SPIRIT IN
ALL MANKIND.

Illustration List

All quotes are by Keith Haring and were first published as follows:

PAGES 7, 8, 15, 23, 24, 27, 28, 33, 37, 45, 48, 51, 53, 57, 59, 60, 62, 64, 66, 69,

70, 73, 74, 77: Keith Haring. *Keith Haring Journals*. New York: Penguin Books, 1996.

PAGES 10, 16: *Keith Haring: The Authorized Biography*. John Gruen.

New York: Simon & Schuster, 1991.